Distinctions in Nature

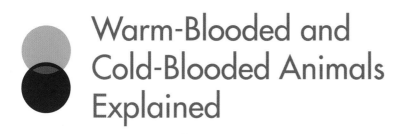
Warm-Blooded and Cold-Blooded Animals Explained

Alicia Z. Klepeis

Cavendish
Square

New York

Published in 2017 by Cavendish Square Publishing, LLC
243 5th Avenue, Suite 136, New York, NY 10016

First Edition

Website: cavendishsq.com

This publication represents the opinions and views of the author based on his or her personal experience, knowledge, and research. The information in this book serves as a general guide only. The author and publisher have used their best efforts in preparing this book and disclaim liability rising directly or indirectly from the use and application of this book.

CPSIA Compliance Information: Batch #CW17CSQ

All websites were available and accurate when this book was sent to press.

Library of Congress Cataloging-in-Publication Data

Names: Klepeis, Alicia, 1971- author.
Title: Warm-blooded and cold-blooded animals explained / Alicia Z. Klepeis.
Description: New York : Cavendish Square Publishing, [2017] |
Series: Distinctions in nature | Includes bibliographical references and index.
Identifiers: LCCN 2016026966 (print) | LCCN 2016029401 (ebook) |
ISBN 9781502621818 (pbk.) | ISBN 9781502621825 (6 pack) |
ISBN 9781502621832 (library bound) | ISBN 9781502621849 (ebook)
Subjects: LCSH: Body temperature–Juvenile literature. |
Body temperature–Regulation–Juvenile literature. | Warm-blooded animals–Juvenile literature. |
Cold-blooded animals–Juvenile literature. | Bioenergetics–Juvenile literature.
Classification: LCC QP135 .K54 2017 (print) | LCC QP135 (ebook) |
DDC 571.7/6–dc23
LC record available at https://lccn.loc.gov/2016026966

Editorial Director: David McNamara
Editor: Fletcher Doyle
Copy Editor: Nathan Heidelberger
Associate Art Director: Amy Greenan
Designer: Stephanie Flecha
Production Coordinator: Karol Szymczuk
Photo Research: J8 Media

The photographs in this book are used by permission and through the courtesy of:
Cover (left) www.phlair.de/Getty Images; cover (right) Image by Deborah Rust/Getty Images; p. 4 © iStock.com/Catherine Lane; p. 6 ArTDi101/Shutterstock.com; p.7 Dinodia Photos/Stockbyte/Getty Images; p. 8 Gene Vaught/Shutterstock.com; p. 10 Lucas Schifres/Getty Images; p. 11(top) Rob Marmion/Shutterstock.com; p. 11(bottom) Melinda Fawver/Shutterstock.com; p. 12 © iStock.com/AnetaPics; p. 14 AndamanSE/iStock/Thinkstock; p. 15 Tim Tadder/Corbis/Getty Images; p. 16 NaturesMomentsuk/Shutterstock.com; p. 17 Shri Bhat/EyeEm/Getty Images; p. 18 maxoidos/iStock/Thinkstock; p. 19 Ondrej Prosicky/Shutterstock.com; p. 20(top) kgb224/Shutterstock.com; p. 20(bottom) Daniel J. Cox/Corbis/Getty Images Documentary; p. 22(left) robertcicchetti/iStock/Thinkstock; p. 22(right) Frank Cezus/Photographer's Choice/Getty Images; p. 24 adrianciurea69/iStock/Thinkstock; p. 26(left) Maksim Fesenko/Shutterstock.com; p. 26(right) ©mediacolor's/Alamy.

Printed in the United States of America

Contents

Panting cools this porch-sitting dog on a bright, hot day.

Introduction: Comfort Zone

t's late morning on a warm summer day. Your dog is stretched out on the front porch. He is lying in the shade. His tongue is hanging out and he is **panting**. Nearby, a butterfly is in the garden. It stands in the direct sunshine, hardly moving.

Why are these two animals acting the way they are? Both the dog and the butterfly are trying to make themselves comfortable. They are reacting to the weather outside. The dog is trying to cool himself off. The butterfly is warming itself. Dogs are **warm-blooded**

A butterfly suns itself in the morning, increasing its body temperature.

animals, or **endotherms**. Butterflies are **cold-blooded** animals, or **ectotherms**.

Warm-blooded and cold-blooded animals have some things in common. They can survive in many different environments. They build or find themselves places to live. They eat. They mate and raise their young. These animals have important differences, too. Cold-blooded

A white-breasted kingfisher eats a lizard. Its diet also includes insects, amphibians, and fish.

animals take on the temperature of their surroundings. Warm-blooded animals don't. They are able to keep their bodies at a constant temperature.

Scientists work to understand the world's many animals. Earth is home to millions of animal **species**. Scientists put animals into different groups based on their features. For example, some animals are warm-blooded, while others are cold-blooded. This process is called **classification**.

A herd of bison huddles for warmth in Yellowstone National Park during the frigid winter.

1 The Big Picture

Some animals can keep their bodies at a constant temperature. It doesn't matter whether it is snowy and cold or sunny and hot outside. Almost all **mammals** and birds are warm-blooded. This includes humans. Their bodies can make their own heat by burning the food they eat.

Lots of warm-blooded animals live in places with all four seasons. Blue jays, deer, and squirrels are some you might see year round. But what if you traveled to Asia? Pandas, Siberian tigers, and parrots also have ways to keep themselves comfortable in all weather.

A giant panda eats bamboo and relaxes in Chengdu, China.

Unlike warm-blooded animals, cold-blooded animals do not keep their bodies at a constant temperature. They get their heat from outside sources, like the sun. If they feel cold, they will **bask** in the sun to warm up. If they feel hot, they might find a shady spot or go underground to cool off.

Almost all reptiles, **arachnids**, insects, amphibians, and fish are cold-blooded. Snakes, spiders, frogs, and beetles are examples. Cold-blooded creatures become colder or warmer depending on the temperature outside.

Zoom In

Most mammals have normal body temperatures ranging from 97 to 104 degrees Fahrenheit (36 to 40 degrees Celsius). Birds usually have body temperatures between 106°F and 109°F (41°C and 43°C).

Their bodies get cooler at night, when the sun sets and temperatures drop. Their bodies grow warmer when the sun is out.

This cold-blooded juvenile black rat snake basks in the sun..

The fur coat of an Alaskan Malamute grows thicker during the winter to keep it from freezing.

2 ● How Animals Chill

When it's cool out, all animals try to keep warm. However, warm-blooded and cold-blooded animals do this in different ways. Cold-blooded critters bask in the sun to warm up.

Warm-blooded animals have many ways to warm up. Some, like cats, grow thicker coats when the weather gets colder. Birds often **migrate** to warmer places during winter.

Have you ever shivered when you're cold? That happens because nerves in your skin and body are telling your brain that you're chilly. Your brain tells your muscles to shiver. It's a way of generating body heat.

Cooling Off

Animals have many ways to cool off. They might find a shady spot. Or they might take a dip in a nearby stream. Cold-blooded animals sometimes chill out by burrowing

A black ctenosaur, an iguana native to Mexico and Central America, opens its mouth wide to cool off.

This athlete takes a rest from trail running. Her body cools itself by sweating.

in cool soil. They also cool off by opening their mouths wide. This lets out heat (through water **evaporation**). Some cold-blooded animals, like chameleons, lighten their skin color when it's hot. That way, their bodies don't absorb as many of the sun's rays.

Warm-blooded animals often lose fur in warm weather. Animals like apes, monkeys, and people sweat to get rid of heat. Sweating cools their skin. Cats and dogs have sweat **glands** on their paw pads. Mammals without many sweat glands also cool off by panting. Birds get rid of extra heat by breathing it out.

Activity Level

All animals are active during their lives. They hunt or look for food. They eat and raise young. Warm-blooded creatures can stay active whether it's hot or cold outside. They can pounce on **prey** in the blazing sun or the bitter cold.

A red fox pounces on food, which it found beneath the winter snow.

Warm-Blooded and Cold-Blooded Animals Explained

A grasshopper sits on a leaf for some needed sun before seeking food.

Cold-blooded animals are more active when they are warm. After a chilly evening, a grasshopper might be stiff. Once it's been warmed by the sun, it will hop about as usual. Many cold-blooded animals, such as reptiles, will increase their body temperature before hunting. This allows them to move more quickly. This also makes it easier for them to escape from **predators**. Cold-blooded creatures must be warm and active to reproduce.

Eating to Live

All animals must eat. Food gives their bodies the energy to function. A 20-pound (9-kilogram) bobcat needs to eat more than a 20-pound iguana. Why? Warm-blooded

A squirrel needs to eat often to generate body heat.

animals need more energy because they heat their own bodies. Small mammals often eat high-energy foods such as seeds, fruit, and insects. Scientists estimate that

Zoom In

To keep up their energy, hummingbirds eat two to three times their body weight in insects and nectar each day. That's like a person eating all the food in a refrigerator.

a warm-blooded animal must eat up to ten times more food than a cold-blooded animal of the same size.

Cold-blooded animals can go for long periods without eating. They don't have to eat as much or as often as warm-blooded critters. Why? They are not using their food to produce body heat. If food is scarce or temperatures are low, cold-blooded animals can slow down their **metabolism**. While in this state, these animals don't eat. They are mostly inactive.

1. Alligators bask in the warmth of the Southern sun.

2. Thick fur keeps the snow leopard warm as it hunts in its snowy habitat.

38 Be an Animal Detective

Use the facts stated about these animals to answer these questions. Give reasons for your answers.

1. American alligators bask in the sun to warm up. They are most active when it's warm outside. Are they warm-blooded or cold-blooded?

2. The snow leopard lives in the high mountains of Asia. It can pounce quickly on prey in any weather. Its **habitat** is often cold. How can you tell if this animal is warm-blooded or cold-blooded?

3. A chuckwalla warms itself before seeking breakfast.

4. The Baltimore oriole migrates to warmer locations each winter.

3. The chuckwalla is a lizard from the southwestern United States and northern Mexico. As the day gets hotter, it lightens its skin color. What qualities tell you if this animal is warm-blooded or cold-blooded?

4. Baltimore orioles eat insects, fruit, and nectar. They feed frequently. These birds migrate to warmer places for the winter. Is this bird warm-blooded or cold-blooded?

1. Alligators are cold-blooded because they use the sun's heat to increase their body temperature. Also, they are more active in warmer weather.

2. The snow leopard shows it is warm-blooded because it moves quickly even when it's cold outside.

3. The chuckwalla is cold-blooded because it can lighten its skin to stay cooler. Also, all lizards are cold-blooded.

4. The oriole is warm-blooded because it eats frequently and migrates in the winter. Also, all birds are warm-blooded.

Mouse-eared bats hang upside down while resting in a cave. They often hunt late in the evening.

4 Rule Breakers

Not every animal falls neatly into the categories of warm-blooded or cold-blooded. Some are rule breakers. For example, bats are mammals, but their body temperature can vary depending on their environment. This is especially true when the bats are not active. A bat's body temperature is warm when it's active, but it can drop when it is resting.

Insects are cold-blooded as a rule. However, some insects can raise their body temperature by beating their wings. Honeybee workers flutter their wings and shiver in groups

Bees change places so all can spend time inside the cluster where it's warm.

A honeybee needs to maintain a warm body temperature to fly.

to keep warm in winter. They also beat their wings to warm up so they can fly.

Nearly all fish are cold-blooded. However, the deep-water opah keeps its blood warmer than the water

The opah moves its fins fast to maintain body temperature in frigid water. This one was caught off of the coast of California.

surrounding it by flapping its pectoral fins very fast and "saving" the heat it makes in its gills.

On your next outdoor adventure, see if you can classify animals as warm-blooded or cold-blooded.

arachnid An arthropod such as a scorpion or a spider; the front of its two-sectioned body has four pairs of legs but no antennae.

bask To lie exposed to light and warmth, typically from the sun.

classification Arranging in or assigning to categories based on shared characteristics.

cold-blooded Having a body temperature that varies with that of the environment.

ectotherm An animal that depends on external sources for its body heat.

endotherm An animal that can generate its own body heat.

evaporation The process of turning from a liquid into a gas.

gland An organ in a body that gives off chemicals that are sent into the surroundings or used in the body.

habitat The place or kind of place where an animal or plant naturally lives or grows.

mammals Warm-blooded vertebrates (animals with backbones) that nourish their young with milk secreted by females. Their skin is usually covered with hair or fur.

metabolism The chemical processes that occur within a living organism to maintain life.

migrate To move from one habitat or region to another, especially regularly, according to the seasons.

nectar A sweet liquid given off by plants, particularly by flowers.

panting Breathing hard or quickly.

predator An animal that survives by killing and eating other animals.

prey An animal that is hunted or killed for food by another animal.

species A category of living things made up of related individuals able to produce fertile offspring.

warm-blooded Relating to animals that maintain a constant body temperature that is mostly independent of the surrounding environment.

Books

Arnold, Caroline. *Too Hot? Too Cold?: Keeping Body Temperature Just Right.* Watertown, MA: Charlesbridge, 2013.

Costain, Meredith. *Reptiles: Cold-Blooded Creatures.* New York: PowerKids Press, 2015.

Holland, Simon. *EyeWonder: Reptiles.* New York: DK Publishing, 2013.

Websites

Cool Cosmos (NASA)
http://coolcosmos.ipac.caltech.edu/image_galleries/ir_zoo/coldwarm.html
Neat images illustrate "Warm- and Cold-Blooded."

Discovery News
http://www.seeker.com/warm-blooded-vs-cold-blooded-whats-the-difference-1792604551.html
Learn the important differences between warm-blooded and cold-blooded animals.

Index

Page numbers in **boldface** are illustrations.

Alicia Z. Klepeis loves to research fun and out-of-the-ordinary topics that make nonfiction exciting for readers. Alicia began her career at the National Geographic Society. She is the author of many kids' books, including *The World's Strangest Foods*, *Bizarre Things We've Called Medicine*, *Francisco's Kites*, and *From Pizza to Pisa*. She lives with her family in upstate New York.